Excellence
in
Teacher
Education

NEA
SCHOOL RESTRUCTURING SERIES

Excellence in Teacher Education:

Helping Teachers Develop Learner-Centered Schools

Linda Darling-Hammond

Gary A. Griffin

Arthur E. Wise

Robert M. McClure
NEA Mastery In Learning Consortium
NEA National Center for Innovation
Series Editor

nea PROFESSIONAL LIBRARY
National Education Association
Washington, D.C.

Printing History
    First Printing: January 1992

Note

The opinions expressed in this publication should not be construed as representing the policy or position of the National Education Association. Materials published by the NEA Professional Library are intended to be discussion documents for educators who are concerned with specialized interests of the profession.

Library of Congress Cataloging-in-Publication Data
Darling-Hammond, Linda. 1951–
    Excellence in teacher education : helping teachers develop learner
    -centered schools / Linda Darling-Hammond, Gary A. Griffin, Arthur
    E. Wise.
        p.   cm. — (NEA school restructuring series)
    Includes bibliographical references.
    ISBN 0–8106–1847–8
    1. Teacher — Training of — United States. I. Griffin, Gary A.
    II. Wise, Arthur E. III. Title. IV. Series.
    LB1715.D34   1992
    370'.71—dc20   91–27154
                                            20   CIP

CONTENTS

FOREWORD

If one accepts the idea that K–12 schools need to change fundamentally, then attention must turn to the need for serious reform of those institutions that educate prospective teachers. Fortunately, leaders in the teacher education community have come forth in recent years with a number of proposals that will be central to the restructuring of programs that prepare teachers.

These proposals have suggested stronger ties between preparation programs and the schools and have called for a more collegial relationship between teachers and professors. The reason: both have much to learn from the other. It has been difficult, however, to define how and what these learnings can and should be.

Several issues have characterized the discussions taking us toward new ways of working together. The setting in which teachers would be prepared is one such issue; territorial concerns, it would seem, have been with us for a long time. Should the prospective teacher spend more or less time in the college classroom or the school site? Should the site where "practice teaching" occurs be an ideal one or a "real" one? What should be the prerogatives held by the various actors as they move from college campus to school campus and back again?

Such questions as these characterized debates about teacher preparation in the past. They had to do with authority, with role, and, most important, with the issue of where the knowledge that would be the most relevant to the new teacher resided.

Fortunately, the discussions have now moved beyond the territorial realm. With clearer understandings about the kind of school and staff required for the future has come a clearer and sharper vision of what teacher education must become. Now, teachers and professors are at the heart of the matter—*helping teachers create learner-centered schools.* Developing schools that truly serve their clients (and not the needs of a system too often unresponsive to those needs) requires a restructuring—*a reconceptualization*—of the ways future teachers are prepared.

This monograph deals with three issues that will shape teacher education programs in the future. The first is the *content* that should permeate the preparing institutions, with particular attention to the kind of teachers and teaching required in the schools of the future. The second is the *context* that must prevail in the schools if exemplary practice is to occur. Here, the emphasis is on the *professionalization* of teaching. Finally, the material that follows provides a clear delineation of *public policy* that will cause and support the changes proposed.

Three educators deeply involved in the worlds of practice, theory, and policy are the authors of this monograph. They have taken what appears to be a complex and intransigent set of issues and problems and have made them understandable. Better yet, they make us feel that all of this can happen!

—Robert M. McClure
Editor, School Restructuring Series
Director, Mastery In Learning Consortium,
NEA National Center for Innovation

Chapter 1

PERESTROIKA AND PROFESSIONALISM: THE CASE FOR RESTRUCTURING TEACHER PREPARATION

by Linda Darling-Hammond

This monograph focuses on the changes that are being wrought by school restructuring, or "educational perestroika" as it might be called, and their implications for changes in the teacher's role and consequently for teacher education.

This chapter discusses how school restructuring—that is, the creation of learner-centered schools—presses for a new conception of teaching and how that changing view of teaching requires the reform of teacher education.

The argument in a nutshell is that if schools are to focus on learning, rather than merely offering courses, then teachers must be able to diagnose and address various learning needs, rather than merely "delivering instruction." They must have the knowledge and the capacity to connect with learners, rather than simply covering the curriculum.

This idea has many implications for how schools are structured and organized to facilitate learning: learning arrangements need to be more personalized so that teachers can come to know the minds of their students well; curricula and methods must be more focused on learners' needs rather than on standardized procedures; school life must be more coherent and well-integrated and less fragmented and bureaucratized. Teachers must be asked and expected to "do the right things," rather than to "do things right."

The creation of learner-centered schools also has many implications for teacher education: teachers' preparation will need to incorporate more deep and wide-ranging exposure to knowledge about teaching, learning, and the social contexts of education, along with more opportunities to learn to apply that knowledge under supervision and guided practice. It will need to prepare teachers to evaluate student understandings, conceptions, learning styles and intelligences, strengths, and needs, and then to construct learning opportunities that are responsive to the learner while true to the subjects under study. It will need to prepare teachers to evaluate different pedagogical approaches and assessment options so that they can choose those that are appropriate for various learning goals under varying conditions. It will need to prepare teachers to understand the cultural and social contexts within which students approach learning so that they can build upon the students' cognitive foundations, rather than undermining them. This is a radically different conception of teaching and teachers' knowledge than has been implicit in many policymakers' views of teacher education.

And, finally, the creation of learner-centered schools will ultimately require more control by teacher educators and teachers over the definition of knowledge as it is expressed in certification standards and examinations, in standards for teaching internships, in professional development schools, and in standards for accrediting and approving schools of education.

Current efforts at school reform, I think, are trying to move the American educational system from a highly bureaucratic system—one that has been governed by layers of rules and regulations, by teacher-proof texts and curricula, and by administrative directive—to one that is governed by teachers' professional knowledge and judgment and focused much more on the needs of children.

The seeds of the problem lie in the basic nature of

bureaucratic organizations. As Max Weber put it many years ago when he was developing the conception of bureaucracy:

> Bureaucratization offers above all the optimum possibility for carrying through the principle of specializing administrative functions according to purely objective considerations. . . . The "objective" discharge of business means a discharge of business according to calculable rules and "without regard for persons." [Bureaucracy by] its specific nature develops the more perfectly the more the bureaucracy is "dehumanized," the more completely it succeeds in eliminating . . . all elements which escape calculation. (14)

Conducting business "without regard for persons" means that all clients are treated alike. This works so long as all clients *are* exactly alike. The worker in a bureaucracy is not expected to make this judgment. In fact, s/he is generally precluded from doing so. In schools, as we have come to learn, bureaucratic management, which aims to standardize and dehumanize teaching and learning, fails to educate many children well.

The new wave of school reform aims to develop better answers to school problems by involving teachers along with parents, students, and school administrators in school decision making and management based on an understanding that simple top-down answers to complex problems essentially don't work.

If you listen to the rhetoric of Perestroika in the Soviet Union and those East European countries that are restructuring their governments and institutions, you will hear precisely the kinds of talk that you hear in the school restructuring movement in this country. The argument is that decisions must be decentralized to the level at which the problems themselves actually occur—that decision making at levels remote from the action is bound to stultify initiative and to misdiagnose the problem. As Mikhail Gorbachev puts it:

11

Perestroika means overcoming the stagnation process, breaking down the braking mechanism, creating a dependable and effective mechanism for the acceleration of social and economic progress and giving it greater dynamism .... [Perestroika] means ... the comprehensive development of democracy, self-government, encouragement of initiative and creative endeavor ... the renunciation of management by injunction and by administrative methods, and the overall encouragement of innovation. .... The aim of this reform is to ensure the transition from an excessively centralized management system relying on orders, to a democratic one, based on the combination of democratic centralism and self-management. (13, p.34)

At some very fundamental level this diagnosis of how to bring about improvement is substantially different from the diagnosis that has driven much of the policy that has formed the organization of schools and school districts in this country. It is also a very different theory from that which has informed teacher preparation and the level of investment that has been made in teachers' knowledge.

Since the adoption of a bureaucratic form of management at the turn of the twentieth century, our school organizations have essentially pursued what you might think of as a trickle-down theory of knowledge. This theory assumes that somehow most of the knowledge about what to do in schools and classrooms resides at the top of a very large hierarchical system. It is embodied in required textbooks, curriculum packages, memoranda and directives, and systems that have been established for the placement, grouping, labeling, promotion, and treatment of students. The theory further assumes that knowledge that has been embodied in those structures and rules trickles down to the classroom teacher by way of the materials and procedures that the teachers are expected to use.

This is not a view that assumes that knowledge needs to

12

be in the hands and mind of the teacher, to be applied to problems that require complex decision making. Since most of the important decisions are made outside the classroom, the teacher's role is seen as that of an implementer, not a conceptualizer. It is not a view that assumes that the teacher makes educational decisions that ought then to "trickle up" to the top of the system and change the ways in which the structure itself operates.

Gorbachev talks about ensuring that control actually devolves to the bottom of the system, in the same way that policy analyst Dick Elmore talks about the "power of the bottom over the top" (10). Elmore's point is one that policy studies have rediscovered over and over again throughout the past decade— that those who implement policies ultimately decide what the policies will mean in action, that they will make decisions in any case, so they should be supported, through both knowledge-building efforts and the granting of flexibility, to make decisions that will work well in their unique contexts (5).

There is a related point: that because students learn at different rates and in different ways, there will never be "one best system" of education, or a singular set of teaching prescriptions that can meet all of their diverse needs. Standardized practice in this context is malpractice. Consequently, learner-centered policies must invest in teacher knowledge and support local decision making to ensure that students' individual circumstances and needs are appropriately addressed (4).

We've had a push and pull for many, many years between these two very different conceptions of how teaching and learning occur and how schools ought to be organized. However, I believe we are at a point in our history where the reform movement is not going to fade away after a few years in the way that it has quite often in the past.

There's an old Haitian proverb: "Ignorance doesn't kill

13

you, but it makes you sweat a lot." I think that we as a nation are undergoing a massive and now rather long-standing school reform movement because we are sweating a lot. We're sweating because our economy and our society are changing at a breakneck pace, but we have not yet reshaped our schools so that they can keep up.

Current school organizations, which were developed around the turn of this century to meet very different needs, cannot meet the needs of the future. At that time, about half of our jobs were low-skilled and semiskilled labor jobs; less than 10 percent were professional or technical jobs requiring specialized knowledge or skill. Now, only 6 percent of our jobs are low-skilled or unskilled labor jobs, and nearly half are professional, managerial, and technical jobs. Most of these require skilled workers, and the level and type of skill required are increasing.

Around 1900, American schools were organized, essentially on a factory model, to process students through a standardized set of educational experiences. Students were to move through the grades, the prescribed programs, the courses and be stamped with a curriculum, a set of lessons. For those for whom the system worked, this seemed fine and good. And the fact that the system didn't work for many was not really viewed as a problem because there were lines at the mill and places on the farm and in the factory for those who left school without much education. Because the economy did not demand many educated workers, there was not great pressure to change this system, even though there were large numbers of dropouts: nearly 80 percent dropped out at the turn of the century, 50 percent dropped out only 40 years ago, and we still fail to graduate close to 25 percent of students today.

Given this approach to education as a form of "processing," there was not a great investment in teacher

14

preparation. Teachers were not particularly expected to develop a variety of ways to ensure student success; they were regarded by the policy system as semiskilled workers who needed only to follow the curriculum guide. We still see this conception present in alternative certification proposals, which assume that four to six weeks is enough time to get somebody ready to go into the classroom to teach.

These conceptions of teaching were not as problematic for society then, at a time when our economy could deal with people for whom school didn't succeed, as they are today. Today these outmoded conceptions of teaching and learning are a major problem. Individuals who do not succeed in school cannot survive in society. High school dropouts have only one chance out of three of getting any job at all. And if they do find employment, they'll earn only half as much as they would have a decade earlier (15). Over the next decade, those chances will decline even further.

Because of the social pressures created by these changes, I believe we will see a continuation of the kind of school reform that is striving to find a way to structure schools and teaching so that they can address the needs of the learner rather than merely covering the curriculum and offering courses.

As a nation, we are now in a situation where we cannot allow children to fail. And we cannot rectify our current failures in schools without having an entire cadre of teachers—not just a few, but two and a half million teachers—who can figure out what it is that a child needs and find a way to meet that need. In order to achieve this goal, we need to "professionalize" teaching.

What do we mean by professionalization? There are essentially three conditions that exist in a profession (3). The first requirement is that knowledge—not opinion, not procedure, not the way it has always been done, but professionwide knowledge—is the basis for permission to practice

15

and for decision making.

The second requirement is that professionals pledge their first concern to the welfare of the client and to the use of knowledge on behalf of the client. So if, in fact, a particular way of approaching something does not meet the need of the client, if it is not successful, a professional commitment requires the teacher to find another way, and another, and another, and another until a method is found to meet the need of the client.

Current conceptions of teaching and schooling, which are based on the implementation of standardized procedures, do not support teachers in making this commitment. As an analogue, if you go to your doctor, s/he doesn't say, "This is the treatment I have available, the one and only treatment I have available; take it and I'll tell you later how well you've done in getting better." S/he works with you over time, often trying a variety of treatments, to find one that will meet the circumstances of your individual case.

Yet schools, especially secondary schools, are still structured such that the teacher's role is to deliver the lesson, give a test, and assign a grade, with very little opportunity to identify and address whatever the problem was that may not have produced success on the part of the student in the first place. Thus, adopting a professional conception of teaching would redefine the entire job of the teacher in many respects.

The third requirement of a profession is that members of the occupation themselves take on the responsibility for defining, transmitting, and enforcing standards of ethics and standards of practice. These standards are intended to support a continual search for knowledge to apply to student problems and to ensure that the interests of the client are always put first. While we have elements of this third condition in teaching today, they struggle against a system that pushes in another direction.

Why does solving our schools' problems require a new

16

conception of teaching? As we've noted, the factory model of instruction, operated by top-down decision making, essentially depends on the assumption that all students are alike. It assumes that a given stimulus will provoke a particular predictable and uniform response on the part of students, so that all one needs to do is to find the one best treatment or stimulus to apply to all students. If this assumption were met, you could prescribe the treatment, ensure that it is followed, and be guaranteed results.

Obviously, the assumption turns out not to be true. Teachers have known this all along, but researchers now know it too: that students are essentially unstandardized, they learn in different ways, they learn from different experiences, and they bring different conceptions to their learning. And all of these factors combine to produce a different teaching problem for each of them.

As a consequence of this reality, prescriptive systems actually *create* cracks for kids to fall into, rather than closing the cracks that kids might fall into. The more highly detailed and uniform the set of treatments specified for students is, the less likely it is that any given student will fit the set of assumptions upon which these prescriptions for teaching and learning are based. And these systems disempower teachers by giving them false promises and faulty tools. This gets to the crux of the issue of what type of knowledge teachers need.

In her presidential address to the History of Education Society, Ellen Lageman argued that one cannot understand the history of education in the United States during the twentieth century unless one realizes that Edward Thorndike won and John Dewey lost. In commenting on her statement, Walter Doyle (9) points out that the focus of behavioral psychology was on precisely measuring discrete behaviors and developing laws that could then define very specifically what teachers must do in order to cause student learning. In its quest for teaching routines and

17

recipes, it was a science dedicated to creating control and predictability in classrooms, rather than making sense of the forms and processes of teaching and learning.

In contrast, John Dewey's treatise on *The Sources of a Science of Education* described a very different conception of the role of knowledge in the hands of the teacher (8). He believed that knowledge should provide teachers with an ability to respond to the complexities that students and classrooms bring, to develop a variety of ways of stimulating student thinking and of solving pedagogical problems. Such knowledge, Dewey said, would *reduce* rather than increase the amount of routine activity in classrooms. It would be used to empower rather than to control the teacher.

But, as Lageman suggests, in many respects Dewey did lose the initial ideological battles in this century. Much of what has been thrust upon teacher education in various reform cycles over this century has had to do with finding the "one best system" or singular set of behaviors that teachers could be taught to implement unquestioningly and unvaryingly.

As we face the next century with a greater understanding of how students learn and how effective teachers support their learning, there is a growing consensus that the old quest for such singular solutions must be abandoned and other kinds of solutions must be sought. What kind of knowledge are we talking about, beyond the fact that it does not consist of formulaic recipes based on inaccurate assumptions about learning? We can talk in terms of bodies of knowledge or categories of learning, but it's also clear that we must talk in terms of how that knowledge is to be understood and used.

I think it is fair to say that there is a tremendous amount of knowledge—both old and new, although much of it has been codified over the last 20 years—that teachers need to have as a foundation for their planning and decision making in order to be able to facilitate learning on the part of students:

- Knowledge about cognition and about how children learn must undergird teachers' choices and uses of curriculum materials and teaching strategies.
- Knowledge about learning styles and teaching strategies that address these different modes of learning is needed to help ensure greater success with all children.
- Knowledge about motivation and behavior will help support methods to promote more successful, humane, and constructive classroom interactions.
- Knowledge about how children and adolescents develop physically, cognitively, and psychologically is needed to design all aspects of classroom life, to recognize progress and potential problems, and to support appropriate decision making about teaching content, methods, and organizational strategies.
- Knowledge about the organization of instruction and about classroom management will help teachers structure students' encounters with subject matter and classroom tasks so that they can be successful.
- Knowledge about effective teaching methods for promoting understanding, critical thinking, and well-developed performance abilities in reading, writing, mathematics, and the sciences has grown rapidly and must be available to support teachers' efforts to engender meaningful learning in their classrooms. And new efforts to further refine our knowledge of subject-specific pedagogy will help teachers integrate their understandings of subjects and learners in ever more powerful ways.
- Knowledge about special learning circumstances and their treatment needs to be in the hands of all classroom teachers, not just those who work in special

19

education. These include common visual and perceptual difficulties as well as a wide range of conditions caused by physical, neurological, and environmental factors that affect the ways in which children learn. Many sources suggest that perhaps one-fourth or more of children in most classrooms are going to exhibit modes, styles, and/or difficulties in learning that most regular classroom teachers are not prepared to interpret, understand, or address.

- Knowledge about how the many different kinds of human intelligence are developed and nurtured (12) will help teachers to see and educate the whole child and all of his/her gifts along with his/her ways of demonstrating those gifts.

- Knowledge about culture and learning will help teachers to understand the role of culture in perception, language acquisition, and learning so that they can forge connections between classroom work and students' lives. This knowledge will also provide teachers with tools by which truly multicultural curricula and culture-fair testing can be developed. (1)

I think a very key understanding that teachers must begin to have available to them is one that Robert Gagne (11) brought to our attention some years ago—that there are many different types of learning, and these, in fact, call for different types of teaching. One of the things that has hampered our search for ways to use knowledge effectively in the classroom is the misconception on the part of some researchers that one type of teaching would do for all sorts of learning, or that the one type of learning they studied represented the other types of learning that they did not study.

We now have a fairly elaborated set of theories, grounded

in research, that allow us to understand how teaching strategies that are effective for promoting recall and recognition of basic facts are different than some of the strategies needed to develop certain kinds of problem-solving skills, and so on (6). Gagne developed eight categories of learning that call for different modes of teaching. Other researchers have developed different categories. The point is that an understanding of how to vary teaching strategies in pursuit of different learning goals can empower teachers to be much more effective with students.

In order for this kind of knowledge to find its way systematically into the hands of teachers, it has to become widely incorporated into licensure standards and thus into teacher education programs, as well as clinical practice settings such as student teaching experiences and internships. You know very well the disjuncture that can occur between teacher education and teaching, because the way the beginning teacher is socialized to a set of practices in the first year on the job does not support necessarily what s/he has learned in the school of education.

This is why many new proposals for internships, particularly those that are seeking to establish professional development schools, seek more cross-fertilization between the school of education and the school site. They recognize that the initial induction period, in which teachers learn to translate knowledge into practice, provides an important kind of learning that cannot take place solely in the school of education and may take place suboptimally if the school does not support a carefully guided and supervised introduction into the art of teaching. So we need to learn how to restructure teacher education to explicitly address the problem of translating knowledge into skill.

What does preparing teachers for learner-centered schools mean in practice? For one thing, it means that the teacher needs to be able to go beyond routines and basic techniques to evaluate which of the various kinds of knowledge s/he has encountered could be helpful in solving a given problem of teaching practice. That is, the teacher in a learner-centered school needs to be reflective and analytical, needs to have an inquiring disposition, and needs a base of knowledge and resources to draw upon in solving problems of practice.

Let's imagine, for example, that a teacher encountered a reading problem with a beginning reader who seemed not to be progressing comfortably. In many of today's schools, the child would be assigned to a slow reading group, and that would be the beginning and the end of the diagnostic process. In a learner-centered school, the teacher would first seek to understand the nature and possible source of the problem. (Presumably, this would be occurring in the context of a language-rich classroom environment that begins with a child-centered and experience-based approach to instruction.) S/he would need the kinds of knowledge, understandings, and skills that would allow her/him to pose and answer many questions.

Is this a problem associated with decoding or comprehension or contextual interpretation or other areas of reading? What might be the source of the problem? Is it a developmental problem? The teacher would know, for example, that approximately 50 percent of students at the age of five do not have visual skills sufficiently developed to allow them to focus on fine print. And only about 70 percent of students have highly developed visual skills by first grade, and perhaps 85 percent by second grade. S/he would know that if a child's reading problems stemmed from such a developmental factor, they would not be solved by increased hours of practice on reading and might be exacerbated, lowering the child's self-esteem (and later success in learning).

S/he would need to know whether there is a perceptual impairment—dyslexia or some other kind of difficulty. Or is it a problem related to the materials being used? their difficulty level?

their ability to relate to the child's own personal experiences and interests? their quality? Are they badly written materials? (Unfortunately that's not an uncommon occurrence.) Is it a problem related to the mode of instruction or to the classroom organization or management? Is it that the presentation of instruction or the methods chosen are not adapted to the child's learning style? Has there been perhaps too much reliance on one or another approach to the exclusion of others that might be useful, whether that's phonics or whole word recognition or context clues? Is it a problem of inadequate opportunity for practice?

Is it a problem related to the classroom social structure? Or perhaps the home does not provide a language-rich environment that would support vocabulary development. The child may be fatigued, or may have problems associated with illness, physical ailments, or side effects of medication. Are there psychological stresses in the home or at school that could impair learning?

As part of this reflective process, the teacher must also draw upon knowledge of potential solutions. This calls for a broad repertoire of teaching strategies as well as a capacity to evaluate how well particular strategies might be suited to particular students and teaching goals. The same requirements, I might add, will apply to secondary school teachers in the school of the future. The days will soon be gone when the profession will accept the old vision of a secondary school teacher as a subject-matter expert who lectures, gives tests, and assigns grades without really needing to understand very much about how children learn and develop.

Secondary school teachers, like others—and I say this as a former secondary school teacher who was seriously under-prepared for her work—also need to be prepared to reach students by understanding adolescent development, motivation, and behavior; learning approaches; and subject-specific peda-gogy. Many secondary school teachers feel that they have been underprepared to understand adolescent development, behavior, and motivation. In many states, certification standards ignore these matters entirely. And I have heard secondary school teachers say over and over again that their complaint is not having had too many methods courses, but having had too few. They want to have more elaborated methods of teaching algebra, geometry, trigonometry, and calculus, and so on, rather than a more superficial understanding of general methods of teaching mathematics (7).

How do we fit it all in? Obviously, the course counting requirements embedded in current certification practices are often too rigid and are not productive for the task of restructuring. Reconfiguration of preparation programs is needed to provide a better integrated course of studies relating many areas of knowledge directly to teaching issues. This reconfiguration, though, is certainly not the sort that's done in alternative certification courses that pretend that in four or six weeks in a summer you can take a day on child development and one on classroom management and a third on methods and thereby prepare a teacher who can be responsive and knowledge-able and professionally responsible for the needs of learners. It will require at least the amount of time currently devoted to professional studies in undergraduate or master's degree pro-grams of education.

The internship year is also a place for certain additional structured learning. All of the structured learning we want to impart does not necessarily have to happen prior to that year. It can be embedded in a real curriculum for guided clinical learning, as in the case of internships or residencies in medicine, nursing, or architecture.

It is important to acknowledge that teacher education

programs often have been constrained by certification require-ments and state approval guidelines from constructing programs that could make knowledge more accessible and useful to teachers. Teacher educators need to be active and vocal in proposing changes to existing regulations, rather than merely responding to regulations.

Certainly all of this cannot be accomplished without additional resources. I think teacher educators also need to be much more active and vocal in insisting on investments in teacher education, which have not been made for many, many years. David Berliner made the observation some years ago that at the University of Arizona, like most colleges and universities, the college invested $2,000 less on the education of a prospective teacher than on any other liberal arts graduate (2). And there is an even greater disparity in what we as a society spend on the education of any other professional—a lawyer, a doctor, a nurse, an architect, an accountant, and so on.

It's not possible to bring about the changes in education that reformers seek without investing substantially more in the teacher education process and in the institutions that perform the work of preparing teachers. The current bills before the Congress proposed by Senators Kennedy and Pell both recognize that fact, and they have proposed an approach modeled after the Health Professions Education Act of 1963 that will invest not only in teacher recruitment but in teacher education as well.

The movement to restructure schools so that they focus more on learners gives us the impetus to develop meaningful change with many more external supports and resources than have been available in the past. We have the prospect before us of creating a new system of education in which we can truly say that "those who understand, teach," and also "those who can, teach; those who can't, go into a less significant line of work."

REFERENCES

1. Banks, James, and Banks, Cherry A. McGee. *Multicultural Education: Issues and Perspectives.* Boston: Allyn and Bacon, 1989.

2. Berliner, David C. "Making the Right Changes in Preservice Teacher Education." *Phi Delta Kappan* (October 1984): 94–96.

3. Darling-Hammond, Linda. "Teacher Professionalism: Why and How." In *Schools as Collaborative Cultures: Creating the Future Now,* edited by Ann Lieberman. New York: Falmer Press, 1990.

4. _____. "The Over-Regulated Curriculum and the Press for Teacher Professionalism." *NASSP Bulletin* #71, no. 498, (April 1987): 22–29.

5. _____. "Instructional Policy into Practice: 'The Power of the Bottom Over the Top.'" *Educational Evaluation and Policy Analysis* 12, no. 3. (Fall 1990): 233–42.

6. _____. "The Scientific Tradition of Curriculum Inquiry." In *Handbook of Research on Curriculum,* edited by Philip Jackson. New York: Macmillan, in press.

7. Darling-Hammond, Linda; Hudson, Lisa; and Kirby, Sheila Nataraj. *Redesigning Teacher Education: Opening the Door for New Recruits to Science and Mathematics Teaching.* Santa Monica, Calif.: RAND, 1989.

8. Dewey, John. *The Sources of a Science of Education.* New York: Horace Liveright, 1929.

9. Doyle, Walter. "Curriculum and Pedagogy." In *Handbook of Research on Curriculum,* edited by Philip Jackson. New York: Macmillan, in press.

10. Elmore, Richard. "Complexity and Control: What Legislators and Administrators Can Do About Implementing Policy." In *Handbook of Teaching and Policy,* edited by Lee S. Shulman and Gary Sykes. New York: Longman, 1983.

11. Gagne, Robert M. *The Conditions of Learning.* 2d ed. New York: Holt, Rinehart and Winston, 1970.

12. Gardner, Howard. *Frames of Mind: The Theory of Multiple Intelligences.* New York: Basic Books, 1983.

13. Gorbachev, Mikhail. *Perestroika: New Thinking for Our Country and the World.* New York: Harper and Row, 1987.
14. Weber, Max. *From Max Weber: Essays in Sociology,* translated and edited by H. H. Gerth and C. Wright Mills. New York: Oxford University Press, 1946.
15. William T. Grant Foundation. *The Forgotten Half: Non-College Youth in America.* Washington, D.C.: William T. Grant Foundation, 1988.

Chapter 2

LEARNING FROM THE "NEW" SCHOOLS: LESSONS FOR TEACHER EDUCATION

by Gary A. Griffin

This discussion will deal directly with school-level issues in restructuring, rethinking, and re-enacting teacher education. Many of these comments and suggestions are related directly to and are strongly supported by the classroom-level arguments presented by Darling-Hammond in this book. In particular, the program proposals made here rest upon the belief that there needs to be a greater, deeper, and more serious knowledge source from which teachers can draw to meet the needs of increasingly diverse students. We must devise ways of thinking and acting in schools that will both enhance the learning of students and deepen the understanding, disposition, and skills of teachers as they work with students.

I have become increasingly aware of how schools are changing, of how teachers are reconceptualizing their instructional work with students *and* their work with colleagues. At the same time, I've had the good fortune to be able to stand back and reflect upon this awareness, something that isn't always possible when one is always involved in practice. I think of myself as being "close to practice," close enough to recognize its tensions, dilemmas, possibilities, and rewards but with enough distance that I don't lose sight of how these phenomena interact, connect, and impact upon one another.

One of my primary sources of information about what

might be called "the new schools" is the NEA Mastery In Learning project. This network of schools from many states in the nation is facing directly the issue of how teachers can become more directly involved in the formerly off-limits arenas of governance, policy formulation, experimentation, invention, and assessment of the effects of practice. Member schools, working according to their own time lines and within the constraints of their own social and political contexts, are creating new roles for teachers and, as a consequence, are inventing new concepts and, in some cases, a new language to support these roles.

In my university work, too, it has become obvious that the needs and conditions of schools are forcing us to think more comprehensively about what a "teacher" is. The Holmes Group urges us to consider using labels such as "career professional teacher", "professional teacher," and "instructor" to differentiate among roles and levels of expertise and preparation. The Carnegie Forum on Education and the Economy has recommended that we think of some teachers as "lead teachers."

The language in the Mastery In Learning settings and in the various reports' recommendations is interesting because it seems to be more thoughtful about and sensitive to the functions of teaching than has often been the case. The role of the teacher is extended beyond the conventional boundaries of a typical classroom, and, hence, the work of the teacher is conceptualized differently. In addition to "instructional leader," implying expertise in working with students, the new language includes "teacher leader," connoting a leader of teachers who is also a teacher. In addition to "teacher of students," I hear about the "teacher specialist," the "teacher consultant," the "team leader." Teachers are also called "mentor teachers" and "peer coaches." Teachers are part of decision-making teams, work in restructured schools, are members of assessment cadres, and so on. We are developing a new set of understandings about what teachers do, and our language is reflecting that understanding.

What seems to be happening is that the work of the teacher is expanding considerably and that the influence of that work is being felt well beyond the conventional walls of what we used to call classrooms. In part, this extension of the concept of the work of the teacher is the result of realizing that old patterns of work simply don't fit new problems, that the schools of today cannot be successful if they persist in the naive belief that schools are simple, uncomplicated places. In part, the change is due to the belief that teachers will be attracted to and stay in teaching if the teacher's role carries more opportunities for taking on greater responsibility and exerting informed influence. In part, we are reconceptualizing what "teacher" means because we recognize the potential for school improvement in the redistribution of intellectual and practical authority beyond the boundaries established by such phrases as "the school principal as *the* instructional leader."

Twenty-five years ago, the late Ole Sand in his speeches used to talk about the "two by four by six teacher." This was his way of referring to the teacher whose professional world was bounded by the two covers of a book, the four walls of a classroom, and the six periods of a school day. Many teachers' worklives can still be characterized in this way. And a large amount of teacher education can be inferred to be preparing teachers to adopt such a characterization as their own.

This trivial way of thinking about teaching ignores the possibilities inherent in thinking of a school's teachers as a reinforcing, dynamic, problem-solving *collective*. Attending to teachers as isolated individuals, each practicing his or her instruction in separate instructional cubicles with little practical or intellectual interaction, denies a school access to important resources that can be helpful in facing and solving its problems,

31

energizing its community, and inventing its future. Preparing teachers for this isolation and continuing their education-in-practice according to its limitations comprise a disservice to the teachers, to students, and to the communities served by our schools.

We have learned a good deal in the past two decades about schools. One of the lessons from research is that school problems and the solutions to those problems tend more often than not to be context-specific. Although the issues in the abstract may cross school boundaries, the specific nature of the issue is determined by the context where it is found. For example, home-school relationships are often cited as making up an important schooling issue. But this issue is markedly different across schools depending on the cultures in the students' homes, the current expectations of the school, the similarities and differences in language between the school and the home, the socioeconomic factors in the community, and so on.

The point is that schools are different; the issues that schools and teachers must face are defined by the school contexts. Teaching and learning, then, are directly influenced by where they occur. Dealing with the uniqueness of these influences requires that we invest our energies and our resources in ensuring that the necessary ingredients for success are distributed within as well as across schools. And the greatest resource is made up of teachers, partly because of their number and partly as a consequence of our recent growing understanding of how new roles for teachers can impact school-level problems. Teachers, after all, are closest to the problems, and it has become increasingly obvious that the farther one is away from a problem, the less likely one will be effective in treating it. A restructured conception of teacher education would acknowl-edge this *and* ensure that teachers are equipped to act collegially upon the important issues of schooling as they are demonstrated in their particular schools.

It is axiomatic that part of teachers' intellectual equipment, whether in a typical school or in one of the new settings noted earlier, is knowledge. Typically, the knowledge dimensions of teacher education are boundaried, like the 2 × 4 × 6 teacher, by a conventional classroom situation, focused soley on the teaching-learning interaction. As we rethink schools as collegial workplaces where knowledge is distributed across the teaching cadre to deal with schoolwide issues, we must also rethink what knowledge is necessary to make that conception work.

One way to do this is to use what we already know about good schools and to infer what knowledge contributes to our notion of "goodness." Good schools have in place, or have access to, knowledge about curriculum improvement, test construction and use, home-school relationships, linguistic diversity, multiculturalism, instructional materials development, instructional strategies, student grouping, and other student-focused knowledge bases.

This incomplete list helps us to understand, given the array of knowledge possibilities that could be helpful in our schools, that it is no longer adequate to have one person designated as *the* school-level authority. We can't depend on that knowledge "trickling down" to teachers. The belief in the principal as *the* instructional leader and teachers as workers who use the principal's knowledge simply won't hold anymore (if it ever really did).

It is no longer reasonable to think of our complex schools as dependent upon the knowledge and skill of one leader. The realities of schooling and teaching and leading in schools have made that point dramatically and repeatedly.

Therefore, we must think of ways to distribute across the people in schools the expertise and knowledge that are so important to school success. By preparing and continuing to work with teachers toward a vision of "teacher" that includes opportunities for leadership, we may be able to attract into teaching persons who will only be satisfied if they see teaching as a career rather than a job. In a career, there are options and choices and possibilities for increased responsibility and authority. In a job, there are few such opportunities. Rather, a job may be refined a bit year after year in modest ways, but its essence remains the same. Indeed, some teachers may want to opt for the job orientation for a variety of reasons. But we mustn't continue to limit all teachers to that orientation.

By increasing the career possibilities for teachers, largely by restructuring the role of the teacher from classroom authority to school leader, we alter significantly the conditions of work of teaching. This change, according to some experts and responding to the reasons that many gifted people leave teaching, may have the serendipitous results of both retaining teachers we very much want in schools *and* increasing the possibility that schools can be more successful than is usually the case.

If these new conceptions of schools as places where teachers assume and exert intellectual leadership beyond the typical student-teacher situation persist and replace old patterns, and I believe they will, it is important to reconsider how we prepare new teachers and how we work with experienced teachers. Interactions with teachers in the NEA Mastery In Learning schools, the dilemmas faced by a number of school districts I've worked with closely, and less systematic observations of practice suggest these changes in teacher education.

1. *Teacher education should pay more attention to developing norms of collegiality among prospective and experienced teachers.* Large numbers of teachers appear to be uncomfortable with, though attracted to, the idea of working together as a *collegium* toward a commonly held goal. Teachers are accustomed to working with children or youth; they are not as accustomed to

34

working with adults. This, of course, doesn't mean that teachers don't get along with faculty colleagues in socially desirable ways; they do. At issue here, though, is *professional* collegiality, the coming together for the express purpose of increasing the intellectual authority required by a school problem or dilemma. This brand of collegiality requires knowledge about and skill in such group processes as consensus building, conflict resolution, having the courage of one's convictions while respecting those of others, confrontation without conflict, and so on. These processes are not typically present in teacher groups.

Teacher education can provide opportunities for students to understand what it means and what it feels like to be members of a like-minded cohort. We can constitute these cohorts early in our teacher education programs and maintain them over time. We can focus students' attention on what is needed by the cohort for group, rather than individual, success. We can help them understand the possibilities associated with increasing human resources. We can provide opportunities to accept the tensions that arise when there is conflict among group members. We can work with them as they move through the tensions. And so on. In other words, teacher education programs can provide future teachers with the experience of group membership as well as require systematic and guided reflection upon that experience as ways to prepare them for working productively with teacher colleagues.

2. *Teacher education should include more thoughtful consideration of schools as organizations, as contexts that influence teaching and learning.* With some exceptions, the professional component of teacher education has two emphases. The first is on "foundations of education," usually presented as abstract ideas in the forms of history, philosophy, and psychology. Understandably, this content is broad in scope, tends toward generalizations, and is seen by most students as unconnected to

what they usually refer to as "the real world of schools." The conventional second emphasis is upon methods of instruction. These approaches to teaching, usually specific to certain subject matter as in the case of reading or mathematics, point students' attention to the "how to's" of teaching: how to introduce a concept, how to close a lesson, how to form cooperative learning groups, how to test student understanding of irregular verbs.

Seldom are students called upon to examine a school or several schools in terms of organizational features. It is even more seldom that prospective teachers are asked to think about how a school's organization affects students, teachers, or the community and what the nature of those effects is.

Yet, we are sharply aware of how a school's accomplishments and day-to-day life are bound to the way the school is organized, how rewards are distributed, how resources are allocated, how principals and teachers interact, what technical assistance is available, and how problems are or aren't faced. (I believe that much of what new teachers call "reality shock" is the direct result of coming face to face with these organizational properties without developing prior understanding of what they are and how they influence the work of the school.)

Teacher education can help prospective teachers analyze these context variables, not in artificial ways but as an accompaniment to their typical practicum and student teaching experiences. Rather than focusing only on what one teacher does in teaching reading, for example, students can interview and otherwise interact with principals and other teachers toward the end of developing an understanding of why reading is taught this way in this school by this teacher. When doing student teaching, teacher candidates can be guided in developing an understanding of the way the school's faculty interacts, what is most highly regarded and rewarded in the school, how information is communicated, and how authority (informal as well as formal) is distributed. What we need is for students to develop an additional "layer" of understanding of the schools in which we place them. And, of course, we as teacher educators need to be more comprehensive in our own understanding of the schools in which we place our students.

3. *Teacher education programs must include greater attention to issues of professionalism.* Although there are many conceptions of professionalism, the one that seems to be present in most teacher education programs is a kind of weak argument for being a "good citizen." That is, professional behavior is conceived of as being considerate of others, adhering to rules of confidentiality, being punctual, and demonstrating other such conventions of commonly accepted civility. Little attention is paid to the professional hallmark of autonomy of practice, for example, and what that means in public institutions generally and in schools particularly. Specialized knowledge for teaching, another feature of professionalism, most often is assumed rather than focused on in public and systematic ways. Norms of professional development and investment in one's own growth as a professional teacher are not required or reinforced to any degree. And service for the good of the client is treated more sentimentally than as an intellectual and ethical issue of central importance to being a teacher.

Teacher education programs, ideally as an aspect of the cohort arrangement noted earlier, can direct students' attention and energy to becoming initiates into a *profession.* We can require self-consciousness in terms of the ethics of what we and our students do. We can publicly demonstrate together our investment in our own learning. We can analyze our work from the perspective of its knowledge requirements and come to understand when we are on firm intellectual ground and where we must discover or develop knowledge to improve our practices.

4. *Teacher education programs must involve students in*

37

thinking about school curriculum over time, rather than simply about lessons to be taught. New teachers are often dismayed and confused when they are called upon to think about planning a curriculum for students over a considerable period of time, such as a semester or an academic year. They have had considerable experience planning lessons and modest experience thinking about the curriculum of a unit of instruction, although even these instances of curriculum work are typically done within the already-established framework of their cooperating teachers during student teaching.

Teacher education programs are woefully lax in helping students understand the intellectual and practical tasks of engaging students in learning over extended periods of time. In fact, serious investment in helping prospective teachers become curriculum workers is rarely observed in preservice programs. There are few opportunities to become engaged with the enduring curriculum questions. What knowledge is of most worth? What criteria might guide selection and sequencing of learning opportunities? What should be the relationship between instruction and assessment? What might guide decisions about selection and use of instructional materials? Students of teaching seldom encounter these questions; even less frequently do they grapple with them in terms of instruction over extended periods of time.

Teacher educators, in practica and methods courses, should focus prospective teachers' attention on students' as well as teachers' experiences with the curriculum. By doing this, the novice teachers can begin to understand the cumulative power of the curriculum for students, or, conversely, its repetitiveness and redundancy. If teacher education students, for example, were to be charged with shadowing one or more students for a year or two as part of their preparation, and were required to record the students' curriculum experiences, they might develop a better picture of curriculum over time. Further, if they were required to use that picture as a guide for thinking about the kinds of curriculum questions noted earlier, they might come to understand the complexity of curriculum work well beyond planning a lesson or a unit of instruction.

5. *Teacher education should give systematic and ongoing attention to problem solving and other forms of inquiry.* If I have learned anything from working with the Mastery In Learning schools, I have come to understand how important it is for teachers in these restructured schools to be able to think through problems, create solutions, and test the power of their creations. The central components of these new settings, as Seymour Sarason would call them, are problem identification, imagination, and inquiry. Too often, in most typical schools, problems are vaguely acknowledged but not sharply defined. Unless problems (and possibilities, by the way) are clearly stated, they remain amorphous discontents, rather than reasons for action. Without imagination, the problems persist as obstacles to best practice. Without inquiry, the products of imagination remain as hypotheses, rather than verified courses of action.

Teacher education, unfortunately, most often presents solutions to unstated problems, ways of thinking and acting that are advanced as prescriptions for practice. It is rare for students of teaching to be called upon, either individually or collectively, to struggle with an instructional or school issue that is in need of resolution, to develop one or several means to achieve that resolution, and then to test out the consequences of engaging in new patterns of action. There persists a notion of pedagogical certainty of practice, a notion that is mythic in its proportions and, in the end, unrelated to the uncertainty and complexity that pervade teaching and schooling.

If teacher educators in universities and in elementary and secondary schools are concerned about preparing teachers for good schools, we will give our students early and sustained experience with seeing teaching and schooling as necessarily problematic situations. We will engage them with understanding the issues that block effective instruction and with creating options that appear, at least conceptually, to be possible ways to ameliorate the obstacles. We will work together, across university and school organizational boundaries, to restructure schools as living laboratories for inquiry into practice, where we can study practice with our students. By doing this, we can create more realistic and effective intellectual communities for ourselves and, at the same time, provide prospective teachers with the tools of inquiry that are so needed in today's schools.

6. *Teacher education must be seen as ongoing and developmental and must be conducted in intellectually sound and organizationally productive ways.* There is a way of thinking about teacher education that is completely antithetical to what the newly conceptualized school settings require for success. Teacher education, in this view, begins when someone enrolls in a baccalaureate program of study and ends upon completion of the program and receipt of a license to teach. This truncated view of learning to teach defies professionalism as a norm because it does not acknowledge continuous investment in getting smarter about practice. It also fights against the need for continuous new knowledge in the face of new teaching, learning, and school context variables. It also flies in the face of research findings that demonstrate that teachers in effective schools testify that they never really learn to teach, that becoming a good teacher is a continuous process of intellectual and practical evolution.

Although school districts and universities offer programs of instruction for practicing teachers, the district programs tend to be sporadic and fragmented, and the higher education programs tend to focus on providing teachers with the credentials to move out of teaching into school administration. There are

40

few so-called in-service programs that teachers believe are instrumental in improving their practice and few college-based programs that take seriously the desirability of building teachers' knowledge and skills toward true expertise.

Teacher education must be conceived of as a continuum of opportunities for teachers to become ever more adept at best practice. (We tend to focus on safe practice. Best practice is a conception of teaching that expects teachers to know and be skillful in the most reliable and tested ways of teaching.) If this were the case and teachers, school systems, and higher education invested in continuing to grow together in understanding how to construct and implement programs of instruction for students, many of the persistent teaching and schooling dilemmas, including issues of morale and burnout, would be lessened.

Colleges and universities must develop post-baccalaureate programs of study aimed at improving the teaching practice of experienced teachers. School systems must rethink conventional in-service and staff-development opportunities. Teachers must demand challenging learning opportunities from both of these settings as well as require that their colleagues, new and experienced, participate and invest in their own continued learning.

CONCLUSION

This discussion is rooted in the belief that the new ways of acting out the role of the teacher in some of our nation's schools provide us with hints about teacher education. In restructured or renewed or improved schools, choose whichever label you like, teachers are working alone and together in different, often dramatically different, ways. They are challenging the status quo, in terms of both how instruction is provided and how that instruction, and other school-level issues, is

41

formulated and tested. They are facing head-on the tensions of working in complex human organizations, places where generalized panaceas and nostrums simply do not work to their satisfaction. They are coming to grips with the difficulties of reconstituting the nature of their own work and the conflicts that arise when that happens. And they are providing the rest of us with important understandings about what is required to do all this.

It is these understandings, this new knowledge, this altered perspective about teaching and schooling, that I believe must inform teacher education. As the schools change, teacher education must change. As the roles of teachers are dramatically reshaped, programs of preparation to assume those roles also must be redesigned. Teacher educators have an opportunity to participate in this redesign, this invention of the future. At issue is whether we have the wit and the will to do so.

Chapter 3

THE CASE FOR RESTRUCTURING TEACHER PREPARATION

by Arthur E. Wise

What policies would promote the vision described in the previous two chapters? I will advance seven propositions that might allow you to think that the conception of teaching espoused by Darling-Hammond and Griffin could actually come into being. It is one thing to hope that teaching could evolve in this way; but it is quite another matter to design and enforce policies that would make this vision the more probable outcome of events that lie ahead.

These seven propositions are in the nature of trends—incipient trends—and, in one or two cases, ethical imperatives, as well.

The first proposition is that teacher education will become more intensive. It will require more time and effort. As an occupation undergoes professionalization, the individual practitioner must possess the profession's knowledge base. Otherwise that "professional" must remain under constant supervision.

Teacher education consists of three components: a liberal education (including subject-matter education), professional and pedagogical education, and practical preparation.

Each of these three components is undergoing change, stress, study, development, or redevelopment at the present time. Some of the forces are progressive. Some of the forces are regressive. Paradoxically, some of the regressive moves may reinforce progress.

Many policymakers are concerned, for a variety of reasons, about the liberal education of teachers. There are regressive moves—like those in Texas—to cap teacher education in order to oblige prospective teachers to major in a teaching field. In more progressive states like California, Massachusetts, New York, Oregon, and Washington, we see the emergence of five-year programs. In these states, the idea is that more preparation is better than less—that more time creates the opportunity for better preparation. Leaders of thoughtful endeavors, like Project Thirty, are trying to figure out what the nature of liberal education for teachers should be.

With regard to professional and pedagogical education, there are such activities as the National Council for Accreditation of Teacher Education (NCATE) Knowledge Base Standard, the American Association of Colleges for Teacher Education (AACTE) Knowledge Base Project, and others that are trying to think through what a new teacher should know.

Some of the most striking developments are in the area of the practical preparation of teachers—the emergence of internships, mentorships, and professional development schools. While embryonic and, in many cases, more plan than fact, these efforts are important statements of aspirations that can be used to marshal political support to secure resources that will make them real. Professional development schools, in particular, suggest radical departures in how first-year teachers would operate.

The second proposition is that teacher licensing and teacher certification will continue to become more rigorous. Certainly, many of the states are giving new attention to the idea of professional practices boards for teachers, like those that exist in other professions. It is a political movement. The creation of such bodies historically has required political energy on the part of the profession that advanced them. Some progress has been made in the creation of boards and in the strengthening of

44

advisory boards that now exist.

The important point is this: teachers must articulate what it takes to become a teacher. Professionals must articulate standards and be in the position to enforce those standards. That is one quality-control development that is well underway.

The development by those standards boards of new assessment procedures for the issuance of a state license is a key development. A distinguishing characteristic of every profession is that it clearly signals to the public at large and to the members of the profession themselves that the novice is ready to practice independently.

Many of the problems in teaching today—many of the problems of the credibility of teachers—result from the fact that teaching does not have a licensing process that anyone believes in. Teacher educators do not believe in it. State officials do not believe in it. Teachers do not believe in it. The public does not believe in it.

We must design, create, and implement an assessment system that does what the process is supposed to do—indicate in a convincing manner who is fit to practice independently. Developments are underway in many states, but Minnesota, California, and Connecticut are in the lead.

Essential, as well, in quality control in any profession is the accreditation system that governs the professional schools that prepare candidates. More and more the field will be turning its attention to NCATE as the mechanism by which accreditation needs to operate.

Other quality-control developments include the redesign by ETS of the National Teacher Examination and the establishment of the National Board for Professional Teaching Standards, which is articulating standards for advanced certification for teachers.

All of this, then, is about standards and about procedures

that function to assure the public that those people who are called "teachers," in fact, deserve that title. Teacher licensing and teacher education need to evolve simultaneously. In fact, in every established profession, the jointness of the evolution is quite clear. The articulation of standards by authoritative standards boards has guided the reform of professional education.

As standards boards come into being and develop their assessment procedures, they must collaborate with schools of education. Standards boards and schools of education must work in concert. Then, one day, teaching will enjoy what other professions have—a measure of respect for the title and for those people who earn the title.

The third proposition, which has already been described in the previous two chapters, is that teachers will increasingly share in making the decisions that affect how they teach. They will operate not only within their classrooms, as Darling-Hammond has described, but also on a schoolwide basis, as Griffin has described. And they will operate on a more macro basis on state bodies, on professional bodies, and in other forums.

Teacher involvement in decision making is critical in order to hold teachers accountable. If they are not a party to establishing the system by which they operate, they cannot be held accountable for the results that they do or do not achieve. That is one reason why the teaching environment must be redesigned in the form of school-based management, shared decision making, and other mechanisms that give teachers a voice in shaping the world in which they work.

Redesign of the teaching environment is also important in order to make teachers responsive to their clientele, and to make them responsible to their clientele.

It is necessary to redesign the job of the teacher so that it becomes a more satisfying job. Many teachers are not satisfied today, in part, because they are put in a position where they

46

cannot do what they believe must be done on behalf of their clientele. If teaching is to attract its fair share of talented people, then it must be a job that is attractive.

The fourth proposition is that teacher unions will better balance their inherent responsibilities to protect their members with their long-term responsibilities for advancing the profession. Teacher professionalism would not be where it is today without the leadership of the National Education Association and the American Federation of Teachers. Teacher professionalism would not be on the national agenda were it not for the fact that these two national organizations have placed it there. Having said that, we still have a long way to go, and both of the unions have some distance to go in reconciling their somewhat competing responsibilities.

It is relatively easy for the national leadership of both of these organizations to articulate bold new visions of education. It is quite another matter for state and local leadership of those organizations to mediate the sometimes conflicting short-term demands of protectionism—which is why, in fact, they came into being—with the more long-term objectives that will ultimately make them a more important contributor to the educational process.

The fifth proposition is that teacher professionalism will demand an accountability system that promotes good educational practices and sound educational results. Teacher professionalism, in the fashion that has been described here, cannot exist in an environment in which teachers are held accountable solely on the basis of standardized assessments of their students' performance. Accountability systems of that nature force teachers to prepare students to perform well on standardized examinations, rather than to allow, encourage, and, indeed, oblige teachers to teach the way they should be teaching—in ways that the previous two chapters have so eloquently described.

Many experts (mostly outside the field of education) today hold out a vision, a hope, a prayer that test developers can design authentic tests or performance tests. These tests would move away from the multiple-choice format to one that more closely mirrors the performance that schools are trying to encourage. If schools want to encourage children to write, then schools should require essay examinations. If schools want to encourage scientific thinking, then their final examinations should consist of scientific experiments.

It remains to be seen whether such tests can be developed if schools must adhere to the peculiarly American tradition of insisting upon high reliability and high validity in examinations. Other nations make do, it seems, with much less adherence to the canons of the measurement discipline.

Let me suggest an extraordinarily simple idea.

Imagine, in a school district, an accountability system that is no more than this. All of the American history teachers gather together and plan the curriculum in American history. And all of the teachers design the final examination in American history. Then at the end of the year, all the students are graded on an anonymous basis. Now, just think about what that does. It brings together the entire faculty to think about the goals of instruction. It allows them to create any kind of examination that teachers can grade. The approach obliges them to talk about standards. And, over time, it reveals whether some members of the faculty cannot teach. For if, over a number of years, some teachers regularly are unable to prepare their students in the fashion that most other teachers in the district are, then that becomes an accountability measure that can signal the need for intervention. (Needless to say, adjustments can be made if some schools serve widely different populations.)

The sixth proposition is that teachers' salaries and working conditions determine who will teach. Some gains in teacher salaries have occurred since 1980. Teachers' salaries are all the way back now to where they were in the early 1970s, but that is not good enough.

Businesses are very concerned with public education. They need to know that this is one place where the market must be allowed to operate. When businesses cannot find enough engineers at $20,000 a year, they offer $25,000 a year. And, if that is not enough, they offer $30,000 a year. When schools cannot find enough teachers at $20,000 a year, they just say, "Anybody can teach, so let's find someone who's willing to accept $20,000 a year."

That is very short-sighted. It creates a process that will surely result in schools getting only second-rate people. The market must be allowed to find its level—to create a balance between teacher demand and teacher supply. However, the market cannot operate yet because states do not have a credible system for identifying the real number of qualified teachers.

And that brings me full circle to the importance of establishing standards, standards boards, and assessment procedures that reveal, in a highly public way, how many qualified teachers there are. That will help to determine the market wage, and will allow the stabilization of the system in a way that permits the teacher labor market to operate optimally.

I will conclude with a seventh proposition. Teacher professionalism will demand more attention to the less fortunate of teachers' clientele.

There are many myths in American education, and equality of educational opportunity is one. In truth, there is a maldistribution of teaching talent in America that deprives the neediest school population of the best teaching talent. Unless immediate steps are taken, it is likely that a worsening of this maldistribution will result. There is an interdistrict component and an intradistrict component to this inequity.

Let me mention the intradistrict component first. Educators know where beginning teachers are assigned—the poorest neighborhoods. Teachers with the least experience are given students with the most severe learning problems. That is very unfortunate for those beginning teachers. It is even more unfortunate for the disadvantaged youngsters who are taught year after year by people who still are learning how to teach.

We must solve that problem. One of the things that can be done is to create some incentives for senior teachers, expert teachers, to be located in schools where children need their help the most.

One little trick might be to locate professional development schools in the most disadvantaged neighborhoods. In that way, school districts would provide those youngsters with the same stability that students in more affluent school districts enjoy—a core faculty of senior teachers who are there both to teach at-risk students and to help train the next generation of new teachers.

The other component of maldistribution of teaching talent, of course, results from interdistrict inequalities. And while those have not been a major problem over the past decade or so, they will become more pronounced in the next decade. Here is how it works. As teachers gain experience in the cities, they have the opportunity to work in the wealthier districts. As those now experienced teachers take advantage of that opportunity, the needy city schools are once again forced to hire inexperienced teachers.

This is a pattern that was widely documented in the sixties, a time of constant churning in the personnel system. This past decade has been a time of high personnel stability, but we are entering a decade of more rapid job turnover. As a result, there will be a lot of churning within cities and between the cities and the suburbs.

The solution is clear. State aid to urban districts must increase. Now, the suburbs are in a doubly advantaged position. Not only do they have the youngsters who are easier to teach, but also they pay teachers more for the privilege of teaching in those nice places. That is what school finance reform lawsuits are all about—equalizing the capacity of school districts to bid for the services of talented personnel.

These seven propositions are in the nature of trends, at least incipient trends. They are by no means assured. In some instances, they are propositions that will be fulfilled only if those with political power seek to fulfill them. In other cases, they are moral imperatives.

These seven propositions are linked to one another. If we can all embrace something like them, we can evolve this teaching enterprise into a profession. The importance of professionalization is not to aggrandize teachers, but to create a teaching force that will meet the needs of the student population, while also preparing America to face the next millennium.

BIBLIOGRAPHY

Darling-Hammond, Linda. *Beyond the Commission Reports: The Coming Crisis in Teaching.* Santa Monica, Calif.: RAND, R–3177–RC, July 1984.

Darling-Hammond, Linda, and Berry, Barnett. *The Evolution of Teacher Policy.* Santa Monica, Calif.: RAND, JRE–01, March 1988.

Darling-Hammond, Linda; Hudson, Lisa; and Kirby, Sheila Nataraj. *Redesigning Teacher Education: Opening the Door for New Recruits to Science and Mathematics Teaching.* Santa Monica, Calif.: RAND, R–3661–FF/CSTP, March 1989.

Grismer, David W., and Kirby, Sheila Nataraj. *Teacher Attrition: The Uphill Climb to Staff the Nation's Schools.* Santa Monica, Calif.: RAND, R–3512–CSTP, August 1987.

Haggstrom, Gus W.; Darling-Hammond, Linda; and Grismer, David W. *Assessing Teacher Supply and Demand*. Santa Monica, Calif.: RAND, R–3633–ED/CSTP, May 1988.

Hill, Paul T.; Wise, Arthur E.; and Shapiro, Leslie. *Educational Progress: Cities Mobilize to Improve Their Schools*. Santa Monica, Calif.: RAND, R–3711–JSM/CST, January 1989.

McDonnell, Lorraine M. and Pascal, Anthony. *Teacher Unions and Educational Reform*. Santa Monica, Calif.: RAND, JRE–02, April 1988.

Sedlak, Michael, and Schlossman, Steven. *Who Will Teach? Historical Perspectives on the Changing Appeal of Teaching as a Profession*. Santa Monica, Calif.: RAND, R–3472–CSTP, November 1986.

Wise, Arthur E.; Darling-Hammond, Linda; Berliner, David; Haller, Emil; Schlechty, Phillip; Berry, Barnett; Praskac, Amy; and Noblit, George. *Effective Teacher Selection: From Recruitment to Retention*. Santa Monica, Calif.: RAND, R–3462–NIE/CSTP, January 1987.

Wise, Arthur E.; Darling-Hammond, Linda; with Berry, Barnett; and Klein, Stephen P. *Licensing Teachers: Design for a Teaching Profession*. Santa Monica, Calif.: RAND, R–3576–MBO/CSTP, November 1987.

Wise, Arthur E.; Darling-Hammond, Linda; McLaughlin, Milbrey W.; and Bernstein, Harriet T. *Case Studies for Teacher Evaluation: A Study of Effective Practices*. Santa Monica, Calif.: RAND, N–2133–NIE, June 1984.

Wise, Arthur E.; Darling-Hammond, Linda; McLaughlin, Milbrey W.; and Bernstein, Harriet T. *Teacher Evaluation: A Study of Effective Practices*. Santa Monica, Calif.: RAND, R–3139–NIE, June 1984.

THE CONTRIBUTORS

Robert M. McClure is Director of the Mastery In Learning Consortium within the NEA National Center for Innovation. He formerly directed the NEA Mastery In Learning project and served as Associate Director of NEA's Instruction and Professional Development unit. Long an advocate for curriculum reform and returning to faculty their rightful roles as key decision makers in schools, McClure has helped develop many of the NEA programs and publications on school improvement.

Linda Darling-Hammond is Professor of Curriculum and Teaching and Co-Director at the Center for School Reform at Teachers College, Columbia University. Dr. Darling-Hammond has written extensively on topics ranging from school reform, teacher education, evaluation, and professionalism, to student violence and vandalism. She serves on the advisory board of the *American Journal of Education* and on the editorial board of *Educational Researcher* and *Review of Research in Education*. She is particularly interested in the issue of minorities in teaching.

Gary A. Griffin is Professor of Education at the University of Arizona. He has served as Program Director at the Research and Development Center for Teacher Education and as Dean of the College of Education at the University of Illinois at Chicago; currently, he is a consultant on curriculum change with the NEA/IBM Technology Network. Dr. Griffin has written widely on such topics as teacher education, staff development, school improvement, and curriculum change. He has prepared the section on teacher education for the forthcoming sixth edition of the *Encyclopedia of Education Research*.

Arthur E. Wise is president of the National Council for the Accreditation of Teacher Education. He also serves as chair of the board of directors of the National Foundation for the Improvement of Education. As a consultant to President Carter's Reorganization Project, he helped to create the U.S. Department of Education. Until July 1990, Dr. Wise was director of the RAND Corporation's Center for the Study of the Teaching Profession. He is the author of dozens of articles and is well known for his books, *Legislated Learning* and *Rich Schools, Poor Schools.* His contribution to this book is based on a speech he gave in April 1990.